books·n·love

© 2021 Daniel Roode | books-n-love
Kantstraße 33 | 19063 Schwerin
Coverdesign: Daniel Roode
Author: Daniel Roode

ISBN: 9798468971376

GRANDPA TELL ME ABOUT YOU

The fill-in book for grandfathers.
Memories and stories of a lifetime.

books·n·love

TABLE OF CONTENTS

THIS BOOK IS ABOUT THE LIFE OF:

THIS BOOK IS A VERY SPECIAL GIFT FROM YOUR GRANDFATHER TO:

PRIVATE: If this book should accidentally get into your hands, please send it to:

INTRODUCTION

As a grandfather, you have seen and experienced a lot in your life. Write down your story and let the questions guide you. Not only is it exciting for the next generation to read your views and stories, but they can also benefit from the life lessons. With this book you can record what you have learned in your life, what beautiful things have happened to you, which people were important to you, what difficulties there were and what ideas you have for your future. In the process, many new aspects will surely come to light that others did not yet know about you.

While answering all these questions, you create a real keepsake that will exist after you. The order in which the questions are filled in is not important, they can be filled in from front to back or crosswise. You can also have a grandchild read the questions, and you dictate the answer to write down.
Take your time and have fun reflecting on your life again.

Sincerely,

Daniel from
books·n·love

FACTS FROM THIS YEAR

It is the year:

You are currently so many years old:

You currently live in:

President is currently:

The biggest disaster in the world this year or last year was:

A technological invention, achievement or other sensation?

This has moved you particularly this year:

That's how much costs, approx.:

One loaf of bread:

A cup of coffee:

Rent:

1 liter gasoline:

FACTS ABOUT GRANDPA

Full name:

Did you have a nickname?

What did grandma call you?

Hair color (before they were gray):

Birthday:

Place of birth:

Height:

Zodiac sign:

Does your name have a special meaning, or was there a reason why
you were named that way?

GRANDPA IN YEAR

—— —— —— ——

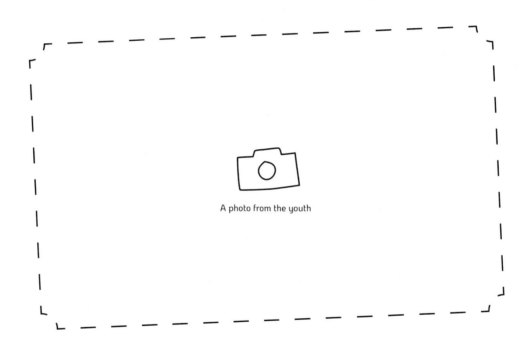

A photo from the youth

GRANDPA IN YEAR

_____

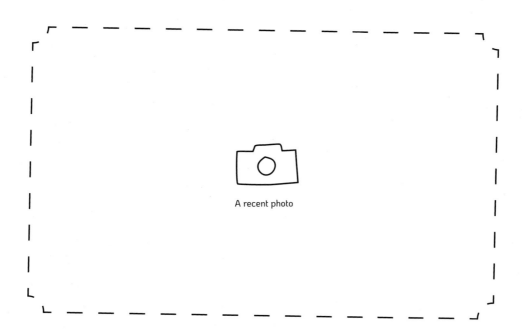

A recent photo

YOUR FAVORITE...

Color

Number

Flower

Animals

Film

Actor

Song

Band or Musician

Book

Author

Season

Country

Dish/Food

Drink (cold/hot)

Dessert

Candy

Game (e.g. board -o. card game)

Sport

Clothes or article of clothing

Ice cream:

Three things that make you happy:

- ■ ....
- ■ ....
- ■ ....

Three things that make you unhappy:

- ■ ....
- ■ ....
- ■ ....

CAREER

CHILDHOOD AND EARLY YEARS

Where did you grow up, and how can I imagine the area?

....
....
....
....
....
....

Was there anything special about or in your childhood place?

....
....
....
....
....
....
....

What was your childhood like?

1	2	3	4	5	6	7	8	9	10

....

....

....

....

....

....

What made you happy in your childhood?
What do you like to look back on?

....

....

....

....

....

....

....

....

Becoming a grandfather does not mean
that you are old, but

THAT YOU HAVE BEEN GIVEN THE MOST PRECIOUS GIFT OF ALL.

Is there a day from your childhood that you would like to relive?

....

....

....

....

....

....

....

What is your earliest memory?

....

....

....

....

....

....

....

....

What did you have the most fun with as a kid?

- ....
- ....
- ....

When were you in the most trouble as a kid?

....

....

....

Did you like to play pranks? What was your best prank or lie?

....

....

....

What values were important in your childhood or youth?

Did you have animals as a child, or did you want some?

....
....
....
....
....
....
....

Have you also had a very bad experience?

....
....
....
....
....
....
....

Were you hit or hurt as a child?

....

....

....

....

....

....

....

....

Is there anything from your childhood or youth that still weighs on you?

....

....

....

....

....

....

....

....

Is there anything from your childhood or youth that you are still proud of?

....

....

....

....

....

....

What did you want to be when you were a child?

Did you admire anyone in particular when you were a child or teenager?

Did you have to do without anything in particular as a child, or were there wishes that could not be fulfilled?

....

....

....

....

When did you become an adult? Was there an event or decision?
When did you no longer feel like a child?

....

....

....

....

....

....

....

SCHOOL AND COLLEGE

What schools did you attend?

- ....
- ....
- ....
- ....
- ....
- ....

What were your favorite classes?

1. ....
2. ....
3. ....
4. ....
5. ....

What degrees have you completed? How did you graduate?

....

....

....

....

....

....

Have you graduated? If yes what?

....

....

....

Do you remember your favorite teachers, and why did you like them?

....
....
....
....
....
....
....
....

What did you learn in school or college that really helped you in life?

....
....
....
....
....
....
....
....

What kind of student were you?
(Did you have good grades, were you studious, or did you never do the homework?)

....

....

....

....

....

....

....

Do you have classmates who made it big? Or friends who didn't make it at all? Did anyone have an interesting or surprising life from them?

....

....

....

....

....

....

....

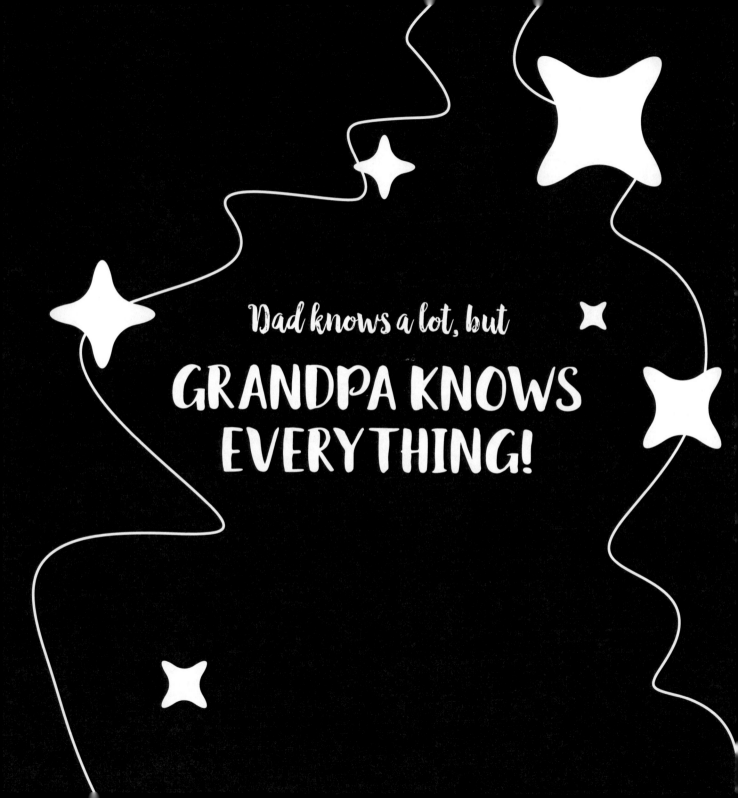

Dad knows a lot, but

GRANDPA KNOWS EVERYTHING!

Are there people from back then that you miss?

....

....

....

....

....

....

....

Are there still old acquaintances you meet today or see from time to time?

....

....

....

....

....

....

....

....

Who did you spend the most time with: classmates? Neighbors?

....

....

....

....

....

....

....

Did you like the way education was taught back then? Were there big differences?

....

....

....

....

....

....

....

....

An anecdote from school days:

QUICK QUESTIONS "YOUTH"

When was the first time you got drunk?

....

....

....

....

Who did you kiss for the first time? What did you feel?

....

....

....

....

Were you confident in your youth?

....

....

....

....

CAREER

EDUCATION AND WORK

What profession did you learn?

Did you learn any other professions or take a different path?

....

....

....

....

....

....

**Did you have other career aspirations,
or did your parents want you to learn something else?**

....

....

....

....

Did you have good conditions? Were you privileged? Did you have advocates?

....

....

....

....

....

....

When did people believe in you? E.g. mentors, sponsors, experts whose opinion was important to you?

....

....

....

....

....

....

That's how excited I was on my first day at work:

1	2	3	4	5	6	7	8	9	10

How did your traineeship go? Did you find it easy or difficult?

....

....

....

....

....

....

....

Who did you learn a lot from? Did you have good teachers or bosses?

....

....

....

....

....

....

....

....

Were you a professional in your field?

☐ I have mastered the basics

☐ It was not a hard job

☐ Nobody could fool me

☐ I was by far the best in my field

☐ ....

Have you achieved all your professional goals (career ladder)?

☐ I was never satisfied with my job

☐ I never had ambitions to do anything else and was content with my position

☐ I have worked hard to get to the top

☐ I was at the top and achieved my goals

☐ ....

What was the best job you had? Why?

....

....

....

....

Who did you work for and what were your responsibilities?

....

....

....

....

■
....

■
....

■
....

■
....

■
....

Did you make a good living from your work, or would you have liked to make more money?

....

....

....

....

....

....

....

....

What work did you have during the vacations or besides school/college?

■
....

■
....

■
....

■
....

■
....

■
....

Have you ever made a big mistake in your job?
Have you always done everything right?

....

....

....

....

....

....

....

....

....

....

The meaning of life is not
to be a successful person,

BUT A VALUABLE ONE.

Do you have a funny, nice or special memory or story from that time?

....

....

....

....

....

....

....

....

....

....

....

....

....

....

....

....

....

QUICK QUESTIONS "CAR"

When did you have your first car, and how did you finance it?

....

....

....

....

What was your first car, and how long did you have it? Was it something special for you?

....

....

....

....

Have you ever been in a car accident?

☐ No   ☐ Yes, that's what happened ... .

....

....

....

FAMILY

ABOUT YOUR PARENTS

Name of your mother:

Name of your father:

Were you more of a mother's child or a father's child?

☐ Rather mom   ☐ Rather dad   ☐ Neither ... .

What kind of relationship did you have with your parents over the years?

....

....

....

....

....

....

....

....

How were you raised?

- ☐ Very strict
- ☐ I had a lot of freedom
- ☐ With a lot of love
- ☐ I always felt neglected
- ☐ Special attention was paid to: ....

Were you favored or disadvantaged over other siblings?

....

....

....

....

What special moments with your father do you remember?

....

....

....

....

....

Name a typical moment with your mother:

....

....

....

....

....

....

....

What do you have in common with your mother or father?

....

....

....

....

....

....

....

....

What is the most beautiful memory you have with your parents?

....

....

....

....

....

....

....

Were there secrets that you had only with your mother or father?

....

....

....

....

....

....

....

....

Was there anything you had to hide from your parents?

....

....

....

....

....

....

....

....

Did you feel that your parents were proud of you?

....

....

....

Were or are you proud of your parents?

....

....

....

Did your parents have special expectations of you?

....

....

....

....

....

....

....

....

How important was the opinion of your parents to you?

☐ I never listened to what my parents recommended

☐ I listened to their opinions but mostly did not follow them

☐ Their opinions were very important to me

☐ I should have listened to them better, but you always know that only later

☐ ....

....

....

....

Nobody tells me
what I have to do,

EXCEPT MY
GRANDCHILDREN!

When were your parents ever really unhappy with you or very angry with you?

....

....

....

....

....

....

When and where did you move when you moved out from your parents?
Did you live alone then?

....

....

....

Did you live with your parents again after that? Was it important for you to move out?
Did you ever live alone?

....

....

....

How did your mother change after the death of her husband, or the other way around?

....

....

....

....

....

....

....

At what points in your life did you miss your father?

....

....

....

....

....

....

....

....

Were there other fatherly figures in your life?

....

....

....

When did your parents support you the most?

....

....

....

....

....

....

....

....

Would you have liked more support from them in your life?

☐ They supported me as much as they could

☐ I would often have needed their help ... but rarely got it

☐ I got along fine without them

Did you stick together well as a family?

☐ We have always stuck together

☐ We have stuck together at crucial points in life

☐ We should have stuck together better

☐ ....

....

....

....

....

Did your parents have a loving relationship, or what was their relationship like?

....

....

....

....

....

....

....

....

....

Did you learn anything from your parents' relationship?
Did it have a strong influence on you and your life?

....

....

....

....

....

....

....

....

Did your parents learn anything from you?

....

....

....

....

What is the most important thing that your parents gave you?

What did you do together as a family?

- ....
- ....

Did you have vacations with the whole family?

....

....

Were there any rituals or traditions that you had in your childhood home?

....

....

What did your parents enable you or your siblings to do?
Any acquisitions, experiences or circumstances?

....

....

ABOUT YOUR GRANDPARENTS

What were your grandparents' names?

on the mother's side:

on the father's side:

What role did your grandparents play for you?

....

....

....

....

Did you spend much time with them?

☐ I have never met them

☐ We did not have a close relationship

☐ We spent time together as often as we could

☐ ....

....

What else do you know about them? How did they live?
Are there any stories about them?

....

....

....

....

....

....

What do you wish you had known about them?
What questions would you have liked to ask them?

Did you learn anything from them?

....

....

....

What one special memory do you have of your grandparents?

YOUR SIBLINGS

What are the names of your siblings?

What did you do with your siblings?

- ....
- ....
- ....

Have you shared much?

☐ We have shared everything

☐ One always got more

☐ Everyone did their own „thing"

☐ ....

....

Did you have a good relationship over the years?

....

....

....

....

....

....

....

....

Did you do a lot together or go through a special time together?

....

....

....

....

....

....

....

What was the relationship like after you stopped living with your parents?

....

....

....

....

....

....

....

....

How familiar were you with each other? Did you always tell each other everything?

....

....

....

....

....

....

....

....

What fond memories do you have of your siblings?
Was there a special shared experience?

FAMILY TREE

Siblings

Siblings

Me

Father

Siblings

Mother

Siblings

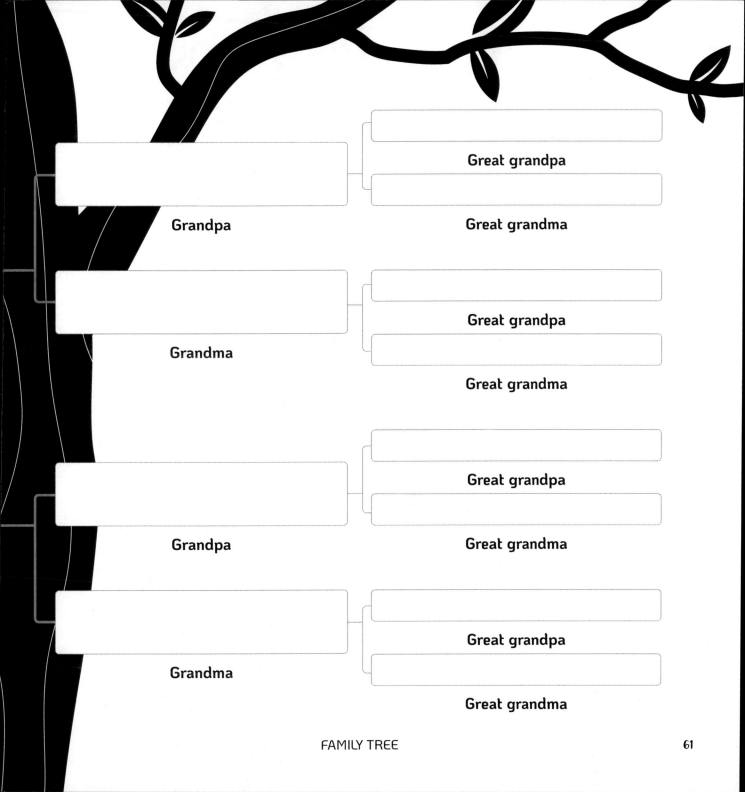

Great grandpa

Great grandma

Grandpa

Great grandpa

Great grandma

Grandma

Great grandpa

Great grandma

Grandpa

Great grandpa

Great grandma

Grandma

RELATIONSHIPS AND FRIENDSHIPS

QUICK QUESTIONS "FIRST GIRLFRIEND"

What was your first girlfriend's name, and how did you meet her?

Were you together for a long time?

Why did the relationship end?

Did you have „butterflies in your stomach"?

How many times have you been in love?

| 1 | 2 | 3 | 4 | 5 | 6 | 7 | 8 | 9 | 10 | × |

TRUE LOVE

When, where and how did you meet grandma?

....

....

....

....

....

....

....

....

Was it „love at first sight"?

☐ I knew right away that she was the one

☐ Our relationship with each other had to develop over time

☐ We realized very late that we belong together

☐ ....

....

....

....

Did something stand in the way of your love?

Did grandma and you come from different backgrounds, circles?

....

....

....

....

....

....

....

What was Grandma like when you first met her?

....

....

....

....

....

When did you know you wanted to marry her?

....

....

....

....

....

....

....

....

How has she changed since you met her?
What do you like and dislike about the change?

....

....

....

....

....

....

....

....

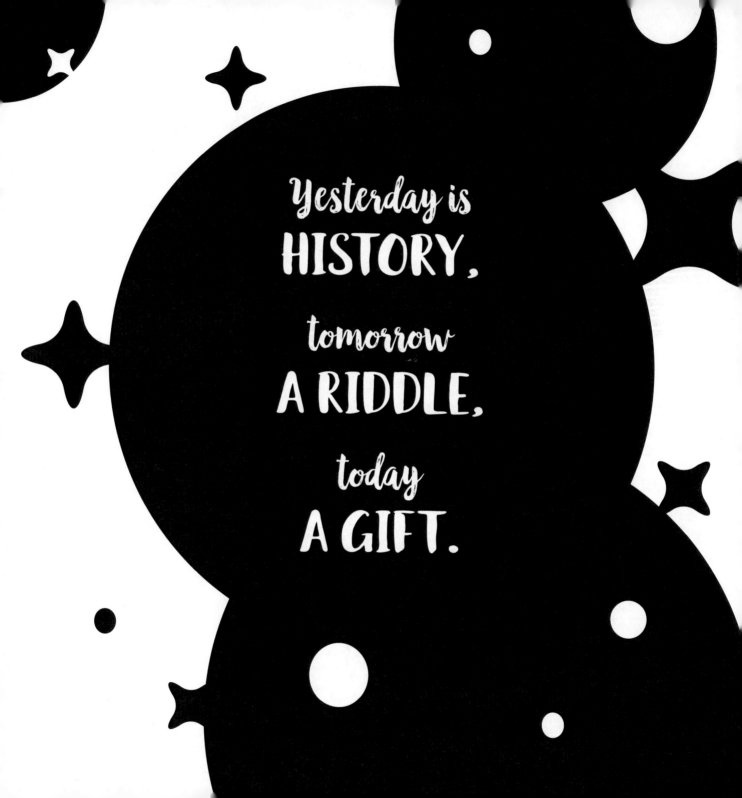

Yesterday is **HISTORY**, tomorrow **A RIDDLE**, today **A GIFT**.

Did she change you? How?

....

....

....

....

....

....

....

When did you move in together, and where did you live?

....

....

....

....

....

....

....

....

What were your favorite things to do together?

....

....

....

....

....

....

....

....

What's your favorite memory with just the two of you?

....

....

....

....

....

....

....

....

RELATIONSHIPS AND FRIENDSHIPS

MARRIAGE AND YOUR OWN FAMILY

How important was marriage to you?

☐ It was a social norm

☐ I wanted to spend my one life with her

☐ It was an expression of my love and attachment to her

☐ Grandma liked it that way and I went along with it

☐ ....

....

....

....

How did you propose to grandma?

....

....

....

....

....

....

....

....

When and where did you get married?

How was your wedding? How did you experience the moments of the wedding ceremony?

....

....

....

....

....

....

....

....

Was there a honeymoon?

☐ No

☐ Yes

☐ We have done this:

....

....

....

RELATIONSHIPS AND FRIENDSHIPS

Is there a secret to a long marriage?

....

....

....

....

....

....

....

....

Have you ever been insecure after marrying her?

☐ No, we have always stuck together

☐ There were moments of doubt

☐ We divorced again ...

☐ I have had these experiences: ....

....

....

....

....

....

Have you experienced a divorce? If so, what were the main reasons for it? Was it wanted by both sides?

....

....

....

....

....

....

....

How old were you when you became a father?

What are your children's names and when were they born?

RELATIONSHIPS AND FRIENDSHIPS

What surprised you about being a father?
Was there anything you weren't prepared or attuned to?

....
....
....
....
....
....
....
....

What makes a good father?

....
....
....
....
....
....
....
....

What makes a good mother?
Something different from a good father?

....

....

....

....

....

....

....

Is there one thing you would have done differently about your parenting in hindsight?

....

....

....

....

....

....

....

RELATIONSHIPS AND FRIENDSHIPS

What special memories do you have of your children?

....
....
....
....
....
....
....

Are you proud of your children or your child?
Did they surprise you in their development?

....
....
....
....
....
....
....

What three things have made you happiest as a family?

1. ....

2. ....

3. ....

What three things have always been stressful and trying in your family?

1. ....

2. ....

3. ....

Was there a ritual or tradition that you carried on or established as a family?

....

....

....

....

....

....

....

Was there a very special emotional highlight that stuck in your memory?
(Something like the birth of the child or another experience)

....

....

....

....

....

....

....

....

Was there an emotional low point in the family that made you very sad or angry?

....

....

....

....

....

....

....

FRIENDS

Who were your best friends and where did you meet them?

....
....
....
....
....
....

Do you have a friendship that has lasted a very long time?
How did this friendship survive for so long?

....
....
....
....
....
....

Did you and Grandma have mutual friends as a young couple?
What happened to your friendships?

....
....
....
....
....
....
....

Who is your equal and can understand you well?

....
....
....
....
....
....
....
....

RELATIONSHIPS AND FRIENDSHIPS

What did you do with friends?

....

....

....

....

....

....

A special experience with a boyfriend or girlfriend:

....

....

....

....

....

....

....

....

....

....

AT THE END OF THE DAY,
ALL THAT MATTERS IS,

how much you
HAVE LOVED,

That you
GAVE IT YOUR ALL

and how much
GRATEFUL YOU WERE.

PERSONAL

PREFERENCES

What is your favorite thing to do right now?

- ....
- ....
- ....

Are there things you used to like to do but can't do anymore?

- ....
- ....
- ....

Are there things you had to do without as a child and are making up for as an adult?

- ....
- ....
- ....

Do you have a motto in life?

....
....
....
....
....

What type were/are you? E.g. nature person, city person, punk, rocker?

....
....
....
....
....

Are there gifts that mean a lot to you? Is there praise that means a lot to you?

....
....
....
....

Which of these characteristics applied to you?

Imaginative   Simple   Balanced   Exciting   Empathic
Complicated   Close to home   Adventurous
Funny   Self-sacrificing   Reserved   Helpful   Calm
Crazy   Intelligent   Playful
Closed   Loving   Experimental
Conservative   Demanding   Introverted   Confident   Creative   Dominant
Sweet   Sophisticated
Mischievous   Perceptive   Imperious   Strong   Tough

Which of these qualities apply to you today?

Imaginative   Simple   Balanced   Exciting   Empathic
Complicated   Close to home   Adventurous
Funny   Self-sacrificing   Reserved   Helpful   Calm
Crazy   Intelligent   Playful
Closed   Loving   Experimental
Conservative   Demanding   Introverted   Confident   Creative   Dominant
Sweet   Sophisticated
Mischievous   Perceptive   Imperious   Strong   Tough

Do you have routines or rituals that you do or have done for a long time?

....

....

....

....

....

....

....

Is there anything you've done your whole life?
(e.g. coffee always at 7.12 a.m.)

....

....

....

....

....

....

....

STRENGTHS AND WEAKNESSES

Why do people like you? What do they like about you?

- ....
- ....
- ....

....

....

....

What do you like about yourself? Did you have to learn to like yourself and work on your strengths/weaknesses?

....

....

....

....

....

....

....

PERSONAL

What do you like least about yourself? What is your worst quality?

What can or could you do particularly well?

What have you always had trouble with?

What would you like to be praised or admired for?

Is there someone you want to make proud or whose praise is important to you?

What are you embarrassed about? In front of whom?

What was the bravest thing you ever did?

OPINIONS, VIEWS AND BELIEFS

Have you ever been a believer? Has faith or religion played a role in your life?

....
....
....
....
....
....
....

What was important to you in the past and doesn't matter to you today?

....
....
....
....
....
....

PERSONAL

Which people do you owe something to? What?

....

....

....

....

....

Do you owe the state anything? Has the state been good to you?

....

....

....

....

....

Did you once think you were pretty? Was your appearance important to you; was it important what you wore?

☐ That never mattered to me

☐ My appearance has always been very important to me

☐ I think that I always looked good

☐ ....

Do people have a good heart - or are they rather bad?

☐ Evil by nature

☐ They have a good heart, but each has its weaknesses

☐ ....

....

What topics are you arguing about?

**How do you feel about money? How important has it been in your life?
Have you been rich or poor?**

....

....

....

....

....

What advice about money do you have for me:

....
....
....
....
....

How important has politics been in your life? Has it had a strong influence on your life?

....
....
....
....
....
....
....
....
....

The best invention, innovation, improvement in the course of your life?

EXPERIENCES

What experiences, in your life, have made you the person you are today?

....

....

....

....

....

....

....

....

In your experience, what things are really important in life?

- ....
- ....
- ....

....

....

....

....

PERSONAL

The Beautiful Days give us
JOY,
the bad days
EXPERIENCE,
the terrible days
LESSONS
and the best days
MEMORIES.

What experience would you rather not have had?
What unpleasant or bad thing happened to you?

....

....

....

....

....

....

....

What age is the best?

....

Have people pigeonholed you?
(E.g. because of gender, weight, clothing, education etc.?)

....

....

....

....

Have you ever been in a fight? Are there people you've had to bow down to, or who don't know you don't think anything of them?
Did you have opponents, rivals, business competitors?

....

....

....

....

....

....

....

....

What was your best or most important birthday?

....

....

....

....

....

....

....

....

What is the best thing you have given or enabled other people to do?

....

....

....

....

....

....

....

....

TRAGEDIES, CRISES AND CONFLICTS

How did you get through difficult times in your life?

....

....

....

....

....

....

....

What gave you strength when things weren't going so well?

....

....

....

....

....

What was your biggest crisis / the unhappiest time?

....

....

....

....

....

....

....

....

....

....

....

Were you supported when you had difficulties?

☐ I have managed almost everything alone

☐ I always had support when I needed it

☐ I would often have needed help and felt left alone

☐ ....

....

Are there conflicts you've caused and regretted?

....

....

....

....

....

What is your advice for resolving conflicts or problems?

....

....

....

....

Do you deal with problems differently today than you used to?

....

....

....

....

....

Did you learn something very late that would have helped you a lot earlier?

....

....

....

....

....

Are there things that scare you?

....

....

....

....

How do you deal with the topic of death? Can you prepare yourself for it?

....
....
....
....
....

DESIRES

What did you abstain from - and later think: It was a mistake to abstain from it?

....
....
....

What have you always wanted most in your life?

....
....
....
....

Were your expectations for life fulfilled?
Or did you have other plans for your life?

....

....

....

....

....

....

....

....

Which wishes have come true for you?

....

....

....

....

....

....

....

....

Is there someone you owe a lot to? Why?

....

....

....

....

....

....

....

....

Who or what are you most grateful for in your life?

....

....

....

....

....

....

....

PERSONAL

HOBBIES AND FREE TIME

Did you have hobbies? Which ones and how intensively did you pursue them?

....
....
....
....
....
....
....

Were you athletic? Which sport did you like? Did you have any sporting successes?

....
....
....
....
....
....
....

What did you do on weekends?

- ....
- ....
- ....

What did you do during the vacations?

- ....
- ....
- ....

What trips or journeys do you remember,
and which ones were the best for you?

....

....

....

....

....

....

Have you ever had a very special vacation?

....

....

....

....

....

....

....

....

....

Are there things you preferred to do alone in your free time?

How many countries have you traveled to?

How many languages have you learned?

Did you like going to concerts? With whom and how was it?

....

....

....

....

....

....

....

....

Did you enjoy trips, walks, tours by car, bike or boat?

....

....

....

....

....

....

....

....

YES OR NO?

Have you ever meditated or had similar experiences?	👍	👎
Have you ever had a real adventure?	👍	👎
Did you have a good work-life balance?	👍	👎
Do you wish you had more time to yourself?	👍	👎
Have you ever climbed a mountain?	👍	👎
Have you ever swum across a river?	👍	👎
Have you ever done anything illegal?	👍	👎
Have you ever been arrested by the police?	👍	👎
Have you ever fought an animal or faced a predator in nature?	👍	👎
Have you ever suffered real hunger (over several days)?	👍	👎
Have you met the Pope or another very famous person in your life?	👍	👎
Have you ever dived more than 2 meters deep?	👍	👎
Have you ever been in a deep cave or something like that?	👍	👎
Have you ever sailed or taken a whitewater canoe?	👍	👎
Have you ever skydived, para glided or bungeed?	👍	👎
Have you ever been in a desert?	👍	👎

Have you ever been in a rainforest or jungle? 👍 👎

Have you ever caught a giant fish? 👍 👎

Have you ever raced a car? 👍 👎

Have you ever experienced a natural disaster? 👍 👎

Have you ever tried drugs? 👍 👎

Have you ever visited a wonder of the world? 👍 👎

Have you ever crossed an ocean? 👍 👎

Have you ever won something big? 👍 👎

Do you like video games? 👍 👎

Have you been to Disneyland yet? 👍 👎

Have you ever been to other continents? 👍 👎

Have you ever flown in a helicopter? 👍 👎

Have you ever eaten insects or anything exotic? 👍 👎

Have you ever „cheated death"? 👍 👎

Have you ever been desperately poor? 👍 👎

Have you ever been filthy rich? 👍 👎

Have you ever eaten so much that you threw up? 👍 👎

Have you ever been bitten by an animal e.g. a snake or spider? 👍 👎

Have you ever been to Oktoberfest? 👍 👎

Have you ever spent the night outdoors without a tent? 👍 👎

Have you ever been in an igloo? 👍 👎

YOU AND ME

What do you like most about me?

What do you think I should work on myself?

What would you like to know from me?

What beautiful experience with me do you remember?

....

....

....

....

....

....

....

....

Have I ever made things difficult for you? If so, what has burdened you?

....

....

....

....

....

....

....

YOU AND ME

When have you ever been really mad at me?

....
....
....
....
....
....
....
....
....

What have I surprised you with before?

```
[                                                                    ]
```

Have you been able to learn something from me?

....
....
....
....

What age wisdom do you have for me?

....

....

....

....

....

....

....

....

When I was a child, what did you think would become of me?

....

....

....

....

....

....

....

Do you see a commonality between the two of us?

....

....

....

....

....

....

....

....

What would be the biggest favor I could do for you right now?

....

....

....

....

....

....

....

....

REFLECTION

If you could travel back in time to change something, what would it have been?

....

....

....

....

....

....

What has shaped you the most in your life?

....

....

....

....

....

....

Is there something that has weighed you down or burdened you for a long time in your life? Have you been able to let it go in the meantime?

....
....
....
....
....
....
....
....

What do you hope for your children and grandchildren?

....
....
....
....
....
....
....
....

What will remain of you when you die?

....

....

....

....

....

....

....

....

What was the most beautiful moment in your life?

....

....

....

....

....

....

....

REFLECTION

Happiness is not a gift
from heaven, but

THE RESULT OF YOUR
INNER ATTITUDE.

What moment(s) in your life are you most proud of?

....

....

....

....

....

....

....

....

Should people do anything differently today?

Was everything better in the past?

....

....

....

....

When you look back, what are 3 things that are really important in life?

1. ....

2. ....

3. ....

What do you regret never having done? Why haven't you done it yet?

....

....

....

What do you wish for your future?

....

....

....

....

....

....

....

What was your best decision?

Who or what has made your life the hardest?

What was your best, most beautiful year?

Is there anything you still want to learn?

What did you experience, try, learn or understand very late?

OWN QUESTIONS

NOTES, STORIES AND MESSAGES

....

....

....

....

....

....

....

....

....

....

....

....

....

....

....

....

NOTES, STORIES AND MESSAGES

NOTES, STORIES AND MESSAGES

NOTES, STORIES AND MESSAGES

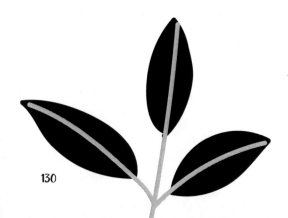

130

GOODBYE

Dear Readers,

I sincerely hope that you enjoyed the book. Both those who filled it out and those who get to read all the beautiful memories. It would be great if this book is passed on to future generations so that the memories of loved ones are preserved and thus kept alive.

I wish you all the luck in the world.

Sincerely,

Daniel

your Daniel from

books·n·love

DID YOU LIKE THE BOOK?

Then it would be totally helpful and sweet if you rate the book on Amazon. This will give it more visibility so that others can find it as well.

PS: Why don't you sign up for my newsletter? I would be happy! As soon as there are new books, you will be the first to know about them.

Simply scan the QR code

...or enter web address:

http://eepurl.com/hFvutb

You can find more books on:

www.books-n-love.de

Made in United States
North Haven, CT
28 September 2023